A DREAM THAT CAME TRUE

A DREAM THAT CAME TRUE

Real life Stories of Working with Celebrities, Sports Figures, and Superstars

CARL J. GASPER, JR.

Charleston, SC
www.PalmettoPublishing.com

A Dream That Came True
Copyright © 2020 by Carl Gasper Jr.

All rights reserved

No portion of this book may be reproduced, stored in a retrieval system, or transmitted in any form by any means–electronic, mechanical, photocopy, recording, or other–except for brief quotations in printed reviews, without prior permission of the author.

First Edition

Hardcover: 978-1-64990-076-0
Paperback: 978-1-64990-287-0
eBook: 978-1-64990-007-4

CONTENTS

Introduction: A Note from the Author · vii

Chapter 1   The Beginning · 1
Chapter 2   The Limo Service · 4
Chapter 3   Corporate Clients · 9
Chapter 4   Business Growth 1990s—New Vehicles · · · · · · · · · · · · · · 16
Chapter 5   Special Destinations · 32
Chapter 6   Business Growth with Local Sports Clientele · · · · · · · · · · 35
Chapter 7   The Greats of Golf · 59
Chapter 8   Celebrities · 65
Chapter 9   First Retirement · 86
Chapter 10 Closing · 89

About the Author · 90

INTRODUCTION: A NOTE FROM THE AUTHOR

A Dream That Came True

I grew up in Lawrenceville, a small steel community in Pittsburgh, Pennsylvania. By today's standards, my family was poor. My father was a steelworker, and my mother worked for a dry cleaner, where she was paid twenty-five cents per hour. Mom and Dad raised five children, while working paycheck to paycheck.

I attended a Catholic grade school and then went onto trade school, where I would be trained for a job in the commercial trades. Coming from that type of background, I never imagined I would succeed in a world of unknown possibilities and enjoy the many opportunities that were afforded to me. Time and time again, it has been proven that hard work, faith, goal setting, and determination lead to success.

This book includes several unique stories about celebrities, sports figures, and some very powerful people who have influenced the world as we know it. I hope you enjoy my story.

—Carl J. Gasper Jr., author

CHAPTER 1:
THE BEGINNING

I was born to Carl and Pearl Gasper in 1946 and raised in Lawrenceville, Pennsylvania. My dad, a steelworker, worked at the Hepenstall Steel Mill.

I attended Catholic grade school and went on to a trade school to learn carpentry. After four years of school and receiving a diploma, I switched gears. I wanted to sell something and become the number-one salesman—I just didn't know what to sell. Then one Saturday afternoon, a Fuller Brush salesman came to our door. My mother invited him in and bought brushes and a broom. I thought, "I can sell that!" After meeting with a territory manager, I landed my first job.

What an education that was! I learned much more than I would have by going to a college that my parents certainly couldn't afford. After four years of knocking on doors and making calls in every large building in the city of Pittsburgh, in 1967, at twenty years old, I was making around $22,000 a year and was able to help my parents with living expenses. I accomplished my goal: I was the number-one salesman in the district.

I had the opportunity of meeting Mr. Fuller in person, and I received a trophy from him at a breakfast meeting held at the Holiday Inn in Greentree, Pennsylvania. What an honor and thrill! (I still have that trophy from 1967 in my possession to this day.) When I had the chance to speak to Mr. Fuller, I asked him, "Is that all there is?" Mr. Fuller responded, "Good job, Carl. Now let's see if you can do this two years in a row." I wasn't satisfied with that. I knew there had to be something more for me, and I keep this trophy to remind me there is always something bigger and better out there.

That was all I needed to move on to those bigger and better things. I soon met a guy who was making a lot of money and working only thirty-two weeks out of the year. He drove a new sports car and had bought a new Corvette for his girlfriend as a graduation present. We got it ready for delivery and tied a big red bow to the roof. He let me drive it to her home for her surprise. This man was only three years older than me! He was a manufacturer's representative, selling ladies' sportswear for a company called Aileen. He helped me make a connection for a line of ladies' apparel; he took me under his wing and gave me contacts to develop in a different price range. After three years of hard work, I earned recognition in the industry and connected with a small Jewish firm in Pittsburgh to serve my apprenticeship in the ladies' apparel industry.

Finally, a New York company heard about me and the reputation I was making in my territory. They made me an offer, and I knew then I was on my way to bigger and better things, like setting higher goals and hitting them—and making a lot of money along the way. As time went on, I became the number-one salesman of an $85 million dollar company called Fire Islander. Fire Islander was owned by billionaire Mr. Lerner, owner of the Lerner Shops known worldwide. Being a Gentile in a Jewish business was difficult at times, but I worked hard, traveled three states, and became successful.

In April 1987, my accountant advised me to find a business to help defer some of my taxes. In other words, I was paying too much and needed deductions. I had a friend who traveled the same territory as I did, but by limousine and with a chauffeur! It happened that his wife was running a limousine company, and he would take the limos on his weekly trips, selling his line of ladies' apparel while training good, professional chauffeurs and preparing them to work at his limo company. This inspired me, and I began searching to for a limo company I could buy. I found a transportation company owned by National Steel in Pittsburgh. Due to liability, they wanted out of the business, and I was happy to help them do this.

The company was called Carriage Limousine. The fleet consisted of six tired black sedans, a shuttle van, and an old gray stretch limousine. The vehicles were used for airport pickups and in-town shuttles for US Steel personnel and their clients. Carriage Limousine was doing about $125,000 in gross sales. Being the salesman that I am, I believed that in my off-season from the apparel business, I could solicit major companies in Pittsburgh, offering these companies and the general public a better way to be transported in luxury sedans. They would have the use of a car phone to conduct business and a well-trained, professional chauffeur who was fully insured and had the correct licenses to pick up and drop their passengers at airports. The company would also have the ICC licenses for interstate travel—all this for a cost only a little more than Yellow Cab fare. At the time, cabs were hard to come by in Pittsburgh and not always on time. A passenger never knew what the condition of the cab would be; most were dirty, with the driver smoking cigars and cigarettes. All this gave me great ammunition for my future commercials, but we will talk more about that later.

CHAPTER 2:
THE LIMO SERVICE

In October 1989, it was apparent to me that sales in the ladies' apparel industry were going another direction. My personal sales, and the company's sales in general, were declining at a rapid pace. The big box stores were discounting prices, undercutting the major department stores as well as the little mom-and-pop shops. These were the accounts with which I did the majority of my volume. Then the phone call came; it was Mr. Lerner requesting an emergency meeting in Florida. At that meeting, he made the announcement that we were losing market share and could not compete with the clothing that was being manufactured out of the country. Then, at the age of eighty-five, he informed us that by December of that year, he would be closing the doors of the company. I had enjoyed over twenty wonderful years with the caring and generous Lerner family. Mr. Lerner sent me and other top salesmen home with an envelope, holding something that would *further our dreams.*

Originally supposed to be used as a tax deduction, the little limo company would now be the main source of income for myself and many others within the operation. Now the real work began: selling, traveling, and having the need for someone who could run the limousine service during my highest-selling season.

That year, my brother-in-law Frank lost his job in the steel mill. Instead of just giving money to the family to help them out, I decided to provide an opportunity to help Frank and his family earn it. Frank did a great job as manager with the day-to-day operations, hiring dispatchers, having a reservationist there, and being on call twenty-four seven. His boys were washing cars. They were getting back on their feet, and I was happy to give them this opportunity. They also protected the cash register, knowing there were a lot of cash trips that we had to keep an eye on.

I was offering executives and the general public a better choice of transportation. I concentrated on working with companies like PPG Industries, Westinghouse, US Steel, National Steel, ALCOA, large legal and accounting firms, all of the local hotels, and many companies whose representatives traveled often to Cleveland and many cities in Ohio and West Virginia. I wanted to show them that by using a limo service for their representatives rather than driving themselves, they would be more productive. It was the perfect situation. In most cases, companies billed the limo fees back to their clients. When those companies used private jets to bring clients into their Pittsburgh office, they needed to be transported on land. A dirty Yellow Cab was certainly not the right option! There were many more marketing ideas that I will share with you later in this book.

In 1990, just three years after my investment, we were starting to be a force in the town. We were up to ten new pieces of equipment, eight new Lincoln Town Cars, two new stretch limousines, two new shuttle vans, and a new garage and offices. We had over $300,000 in gross sales, putting all profits back in to help us with hiring more employees and making capital investments to grow and maintain the volume. I believed in building a strong team, treating employees right, giving rewards for a good job, promoting hard work, setting goals, implementing smart marketing, providing good professional service and clean cars, and always being fifteen minutes early to perform the service as requested. These things contributed to our success.

I began consulting with Gil Lucas. He pushed me forward, saying, "Carl, you're a good salesman. I will help you to open doors, get you in front of the right people, and get you the tools to be successful in the sports industry."

Gil started out by introducing me to Mark Barash, the general manager at WPXI-TV (formerly known as WIIC-TV), Channel 11 in Pittsburgh. I began working with Mark and many of the announcers at the station, including Sam Nover and Kevin Benson, and former Pittsburgh Pirates Jim

Rooker and Steve Blass. I soon began to barter my services in exchange for air time and assistance to produce a three-minute video that I could use to promote my business. With this video, I would show potential customers how the limo company could provide service to them.

Next came the introduction to other TV and radio stations. I now had a baseline contract that could be tweaked for other businesses and adjusted to highlight the specific services that each client needed.

JOHN CIGNA

I soon began working with personalities from different stations, including news anchors Bob Pompeani and Rob Pratte of KDKA-TV. John Cigna, a KDKA radio talk show host, promoted my business every day during his morning drive show. At WTAE-TV, Channel 4, I worked with Bill Hillgrove, the voice of Carriage Limousine, and other well-known associates including Myron Cope, Dick Groat, Guy Junker, and Stan Savern, all of whom used my services based upon the contractual arrangement I had with the stations. This was a great move because when these personalities were on the air, I would always get a positive plug to help build my brand name. My service was always available to drive people home safely after a night of celebrating. Everyone was happy to help promote my business and services.

One particularly interesting incident from the early days comes to mind. A gentleman in the public eye, well recognized on television, has allowed me to share one of many limo stories included in this book.

As everyone knows, there is always one person who will take advantage when the right situation presents itself. This happened when I got a call from a well-known anchor at one of the stations. He ordered a stretch limousine stocked with two bottles of champagne. He arranged for a pickup at 9:00 p.m. to take place at the first rest stop on Route I-79 coming out of Pittsburgh. He requested a particular chauffeur for confidentiality and privacy. Of course, we filled his request.

The following day, I brought the driver into my office and asked about his trip. Swearing me to secrecy, he continued with this story. As he arrived on-site, the client said, "I will be meeting two lovely young ladies. I want you to drive down Route I-79 to Route I-70 West. Circle around Wheeling, West Virginia, and back to the original pickup spot."

The driver waited until the other passengers arrived, and then with the divider up and the music playing, the trip began. My driver said for the first ten miles, there was a lot of movement coming from the rear of the car. With the music playing loudly, it seemed like there was a party going on. However, shortly afterward, it quieted down for several miles. As the driver approached the circle around West Virginia and started back toward the turnoff point, once again, a lot movement was coming from the rear of the car, along with an increased volume of the music. At the conclusion of the trip, the women exited to their cars, and they were on their ways. The client gave the driver a very generous tip! Two weeks later, here we go with the same request. We did the trip with the same clients, and my driver said it was like an instant replay of the prior trip.

Soon after, I met with this gentleman at a special sporting event. I informed him that he couldn't continue under the arrangement that we had with the station, and any other personal trips would be on him. He was fine with this and continued to use our service. But I had to ask the question, "How did you ever come up with this idea?"

His answer was, "You know, being a married man and very much in the public eye, if someone would see me checking into a local hotel for a short visit, I would be in big trouble. With that being said, I thought the best way to have a little fun in my life with no cameras would be in a moving motel like your limousine."

I then thanked him for his business and reassured him our business was private and confidential. As you read on, you'll find many more, great limo stories.

CHAPTER 3:

CORPORATE CLIENTS

With this type of support and media exposure from my three-minute video, I felt very confident. I put on my three-piece, pinstripe suit, button-down collar shirt, striped tie, and well-shined shoes and was ready to roll! (It almost felt like I was back in my Fuller Brush days all over again.) Off I went, right into the corporate office of US Steel in downtown Pittsburgh, and I asked to see the director of transportation. I was meet by a very nice receptionist who explained that I must call for an appointment. I said, "I can't ask for an appointment with someone when I don't know their name." At this time, a gentleman walked in and asked if there was a problem. I explained what was going on, and then he responded.

He said, "I'm the director of transportation, and you must call first. You just can't walk into US Steel's corporate offices." And with that, I started doing what I was there to do: *sell*. I had to convince him to give me fifteen minutes of his time to watch my promo video. He agreed to that but not one minute more.

We then walked down a long hallway to a corporate board room with a big-screen TV. Now it was show time! After viewing the video with him, I explained who we were and what we could provide for their executive travelers. For example, I asked when they send one of their private $5 million jets out to bring clients to town, how did they transport them to the corporate offices in downtown Pittsburgh? I also asked how they arranged ground transportation for board meetings, golfing events, and other situations. He told me that they had an arrangement with Yellow Cab. I had just shown him a video, comparing my services to other means of transportation and depicting a Yellow Cab!

I told him that I would perform a better and much more professional service at a reasonable price, and just for his listening to my proposal, I offered to extend any ground transportation service to US Steel employees for one month on me. Obviously, he accepted this offer.

Starting the next day, they ran us ragged with airport drop-offs and pickups, as well as downtown shuttles and so forth. We never missed a beat. After two weeks of service, while I was sitting in my office, one of the reservationists I had assigned to this account came in to tell me that Mr. Roderick, the CEO of US Steel, needed to be picked up at 5:30 a.m. and taken to their private jet at Allegheny County Airport. I said I would do it.

I prepared my chauffeur attire—black blazer, gray slacks, shined shoes, gray-and-black striped tie, white shirt—and attached my Carriage Limousine name tag to the blazer. The next day at 5:15 a.m., I was at his home with a clean car and the morning newspaper, ready to go. I then drove him to the US Steel hangar, engaging in no conversation and doing my job as a professional would do. As he left the car, he informed me that his secretary would arrange for his return pickup, and off he went. He never knew I was the owner of the company, and I wanted it that way.

Later that day, his secretary called the office, giving us short notice to pick him up. I quickly changed into my chauffeur attire and was soon back at their hangar waiting for him to arrive. Upon his arrival he requested that I make several stops and also to drive him to a meeting, which would take part of the evening. I was happy to accommodate him. After his busy day, I dropped him off, and he gave me a generous tip. I immediately refused this, but he insisted and complimented the service, still having no knowledge I was the owner. *Mission accomplished.*

Much to my surprise, the following day I got a call from the director of transportation, inviting me to have lunch with Mr. Roderick at the very prestigious Duquesne Club. I accepted. I was impressed and looking for good news. Not knowing what to expect, I dressed in my regular business attire.

As I walked into the room, Mr. Roderick stood up and said, "You were my personal chauffeur! While you were doing it all, why didn't you tell that you were the owner?"

I responded, "I wanted to meet you, and I accomplished that!" As lunch progressed, he and the director of transportation told me that they were very pleased and impressed with the complimentary services we had provided. He had received great reviews from their employees, but the most important review came from the man sitting across from me.

As lunch went on, Mr. Roderick advised his staff that as of that moment, Carriage Limousine was their exclusive transportation company. This was an annual contract with an automatic renewal clause, expecting no discounts, and the two weeks of complimentary service was to be billed. We shook hands, and his administrative assistant knew what to do from there.

A moment to remember: As we were leaving, I asked for one more thing. Looking at the very surprised CEO, I thought he was probably wondering, *What else could you possibly ask for?* I asked, "Mr. Roderick, would you please, on your stationery, personally recommend our company and announce us as the official transportation company of US Steel?" He looked at his administrative assistant and said, "She will handle it." The letter was on my fax machine when I got back in my office.

I had over fifty copies made of that letter. I knew it would show creditability for my company. Getting an endorsement from US Steel and a very well-respected CEO like Mr. Roderick would go a long way. This added another sales tool for me to use in the market, and it would help to build my brand. I knew I could give a better choice of transportation to corporations and the public. I knew I was on my way to bigger and better things. I was setting goals and reaching them with hard work, building a team environment, and providing an on-time and professional transportation service.

SONY TRANSPORTATION

In the early 1990s, we received a very interesting call for transportation needs. In the scheme of things, this became one of my largest single-day movements.

My administrative assistant, Gail, received a phone call from a company that arranged transportation needs for Sony's VIPs. Upon the arrival of the Sony 747 jet landing at Corporate Jets, located at the Greater Pittsburgh International Airport, two helicopters were waiting. The first helicopter was to transport the chairman of the board, Mr. Howard Singer, and the second helicopter was for the president, Mr. Norio Ohga. Both men were accompanied by accountants, attorneys, and their own security details. We arranged to have two helicopters transport the executives to the Sony plant in New Stanton, Pennsylvania. The helicopters would stay onsite, and at the conclusion of the meetings, the executives would be flown back to Pittsburgh, where they would enjoy dinner at the distinguished Duquesne Club with the mayor and local officials.

I made a call to my contact at Channel 11, who was able to help me get the necessary permission to land at the station's heliport, which was the closest place available to the city. As of 4:00 p.m., we were requested to dispatch two black stretch limousines to the heliport to await the arrival of the Sony party. We would then transport them to the Duquesne Club. Later that evening after their dinner, we transported the Sony party back to Corporate Jets at the Greater Pittsburgh International Airport, where they boarded the Sony corporate 747 jet to be on their way.

Shortly after this visit, their chairman, Howard Singer, sent a letter to me complimenting Carriage Limousine for the professional service that was rendered that day. He also informed me that any future transports to Pittsburgh or the New Stanton plant would be handled by Carriage Limousine.

In the fourteen years of owning the company, this was the largest single-day movement we ever experienced.

TRUMP PLAZA HOTEL AND CASINO

Donald Trump

President's campaign hat

In the mid-1990s, I received a phone call from Norma Foerderer, the assistant to the president of the Trump Organization, informing me that I would be receiving a phone call from Mr. Quin Marcone from Trump Plaza Hotel and Casino. Mr. Marcone called, introducing himself as my contact person. It was his understanding that I would be interested in transporting high rollers to Atlantic City from western Pennsylvania and neighboring states (e.g., West Virginia and Ohio). He asked that I put together a proposal for transportation that included leaving my office, picking up the clients, and driving across the state on I-80. Upon arrival in Atlantic City, the client would be greeted by one of the casino's representatives. Mr. Marcone would arrange accommodations for my chauffeur, which included room and board, and supply them with a beeper. They were to be on twenty-four-hour call whenever the client had the need to use the limousine. When the client elected to depart, the driver would transport the client to their place of origin.

After more discussion with Mr. Marcone, it was mentioned that they had done research to learn that there were several high rollers who would enjoy coming to Atlantic City, but they didn't like to fly. They felt our transportation services would be a perfect fit.

After further review of their needs, I sent a proposal to the Trump Organization, outlining the details and hoping it provided the services they requested. The fee would be determined by the individual needs of their client. The proposal was accepted.

Upon receiving the first phone call for this contract, I felt it necessary to make the trip myself as the chauffeur. I put my chauffeur attire on, stocked the car per the client's request, and proceeded to Erie, Pennsylvania, to pick up the first client with his female companion. We then continued on to Atlantic City. It was great to meet Quin in person and finalize our contract.

After our meeting, I asked if I could meet the dynamic Mr. Donald Trump. He said, "I'll see what I can do." Later that day, Quin set up a breakfast meeting at 6:00 a.m. in the penthouse.

I arrived at 5:45 a.m., very excited to meet Mr. Trump. I feel that I'm one of his biggest fans. I looked forward to meeting the man who had written several books, including *The Art of the Deal*. I enjoyed that book and have used many of his negotiating skills.

As I entered the room, I was greeted by Mr. Trump. He stated he was looking for a long-term relationship for transporting clients to his casino. He asked me a lot about my company and my personal background, and what had made me decide to get into the limousine business. In the time we spent, we discussed many different subjects. I felt like a sponge, trying to absorb everything that time would allow during that breakfast meeting.

Little did I know that the man I was sitting across from would one day be the forty-fifth president of the United States!

My personal experience with working with the finely tuned Trump Organization was great. We made several trips, and my chauffeurs were always anxious to have the opportunity to make the Atlantic City trips. When we billed the Trump Organization, the ink had hardly dried on the invoices before the checks were deposited into our account.

CHAPTER 4:

BUSINESS GROWTH 1990S— NEW VEHICLES

A couple of years after purchasing the company, I was very happy with the increase in sales; however, I realized that there had to be more growth. I wanted to explore the possibility of taking the company from $125,000 in annual sales in 1987 to about $350,000 per year in 1990. After a lot of research, I learned that there was an annual limousine show, alternating each year between an East Coast and West Coast location. In 1989, my manager and I attended the show at the Atlantic City Convention Center. This show gave me the opportunity to network with limousine companies throughout the United States. These limo companies would use my door-to-door services for their clients who were traveling to Pittsburgh, and in turn, I would use their services for my clients when they visited other areas. All of this would be handled at a commissioned rate.

The limousine shows were created for small businesses like mine. They provided information on how to market and train chauffeurs, offering many seminars and classes to give direction for success in your area. My manager and I attended a two-day seminar on professional chauffeuring dos and don'ts, such as dispatching, car cleaning, driving experience, and safety in transporting the customer from point A to point B. There was also a lot of opportunity to see the new models that were available in the industry (e.g., darkened-window sedans for privacy, airport services, and different types of stretch limousines for the corporate world, weddings, and special occasions). When we left that Atlantic City convention, we had so much more knowledge about handling the business and growing in a professional manner. We also learned how to capture more of the corporate and fun events business, where traveling by limousine would provide an upscale and more memorable experience.

The following year, my manager and I were invited by Crystal Coach, the largest limousine and coach builder on the West Coast, to attend the 1990 limousine show at the Las Vegas Convention Center. The show in Las Vegas was so much larger, with many more choices of vehicles and marketing ideas that I could use to enhance my business. At the conclusion of the show, Crystal Coach flew us to the factory in Anaheim, California, to see how the limousines were built, with the hope to sell us a couple. After we had seen the quality of the limousines and the way these were constructed, the car was split in half, letting us have an opportunity to design the amenities for the stretch interior part of the car. A television, VCR, stereo system, wet bar, sunroof, and intimate lighting could be added.

I was very impressed that these cars could be built and personalized in three to four weeks and then shipped cross-country to Pittsburgh. I made a phone call to my financial institution in Pittsburgh to secure a large line of credit. Then I made a commitment to purchase six stretch limos—two black six-passenger limos, and four white, eight-to-ten-person-capacity limos—spending close to half a million dollars. These were all the new rounded-style vehicles to which Lincoln changed in 1990, and they would be shipped to Pittsburgh in time for the wedding and prom seasons.

On the first of April, Crystal Coach flew me to their plant to make sure that all cars were manufactured to my personal design and then prepared these vehicles to travel cross-country to arrive in Pittsburgh. On that special day we all know, April 15, I had arranged with Channel 11 to film the new limos coming through the Fort Pitt tunnels and arriving at my building on the South Side of Pittsburgh. What a sight it was to see! Channel 11 filmed the cars coming off the truck, filming several commercials with Sam Nover doing the voiceover. Sam made people aware, explaining, "The new arrivals to the number-one limousine company in Pittsburgh, Carriage Limousine. These are available for whatever occasions are on your mind. Please call our 800 number."

I had one of the older-model limousines in my fleet, burgundy in color. With the older body style, it was always the last stretch to go out of the garage. It was time for a change. I sought out the company from Fort Lauderdale, Florida, that was converting the old Lincoln models into specialty cars like the Excalibur. Over the winter months, I sent that burgundy car to Florida for a makeover. The front and back ends of the car were removed, and "the look" appeared: white in color, gold trim and rims, strictly for special events like parades and weddings.

WPXI Holiday Parade

Excalibur
(also front page cover)

When the new vehicle, the Excalibur, was brought back to Pittsburgh and added to my fleet, I met with WPXI's marketing director, Mark Barish. Since Carriage Limousine was the official transportation service for Channel 11, they decided to use the new Excalibur to drive the parade

A Dream That Came True

marshals and celebrities in the annual WPXI Holiday Parade. This parade was always held in downtown Pittsburgh on the Saturday after Thanksgiving and was one of the largest parades in Pittsburgh.

Lots of great exposure came my way after viewers saw the Excalibur, and there was tremendous excitement with my employees and my marketing team. The best marketing tool was to have the cars visible on the streets at special events.

I had the opportunity to meet many celebrities, including Alan Thicke, Pat Boone, John Bennet Perry, Miss Pennsylvania USA Kendra Bernosky, Ray Combs, and Elvira.

David Copperfield

The Pointer Sisters

The McGuire Sisters

AL MARTINO

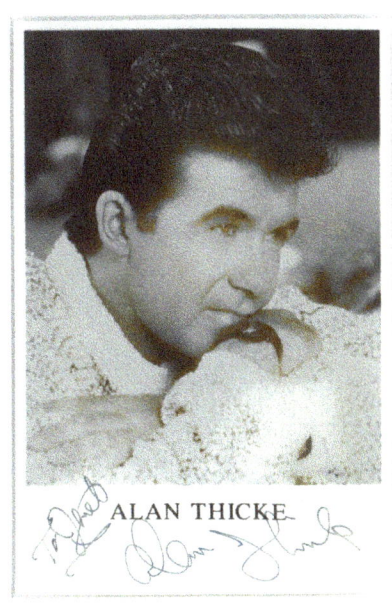

ALAN THICKE

STARS FROM FRASIER

MISS PENNSYLVANIA USA KENDRA BERNOSKY

A Dream That Came True

Ray Combs, comedian and host of *Family Feud*

Michael Vale, "Fred the Baker" of the Dunkin' Donuts commercials

PAT BOONE

We also provided transportation for many celebrities who appeared at Pittsburgh's most well-known theaters, Heinz Hall, Pittsburgh Public Theater, and the Benedum.

JAMIE FOXX

A Dream That Came True

Ray Charles

Bill Cosby

"MR. LAS VEGAS," WAYNE NEWTON

LAS VEGAS PERFORMERS

A Dream That Came True

Brian James

Jerry Clower

JENNY JONES

Jenny Jones

This type of television and media exposure was a major part of building my dream. It was more than I could ever imagine.

As the business was growing, the need for a new form of transportation was hitting the market. In 1993, I called upon Crystal Coach, which was adding the limo bus to their line. Wanting to be the first in the city to have this vehicle available as the market started to change, I asked them to build two limo buses to my design, with a riding capacity of sixteen to eighteen passengers. These would include two large televisions with VCR capabilities, sunroofs, separate bars, special lighting, large luggage compartments for any overnight events, and an unbelievable sound system located under the televisions. These vehicles would be used for large wedding parties; bachelor parties; overnight golf trips; tours through the Festival of Lights in Wheeling, West Virginia; and the Hartwood Acres Christmas display of lights, and occasionally for shuttling large groups from restaurants to the Cultural District. They were well accepted in the Pittsburgh market, but the price tag was hard to justify. These limo buses offered my customers and clients a different form of transportation and services.

Wanting better exposure for the stretch limousines on the streets, I was made aware that a few of the finer restaurants, including The Common Plea and The Carlton, were losing business to the Cultural District, which was exploding with more restaurants and parking garages. I met with John Barsotti, the owner of The Common Plea, and Kevin Joyce, the managing partner of The Carlton, brainstorming an idea that would include providing their customers with free limousine service to and from the Cultural District for after-dinner shows and events. It was my understanding that we could distribute business cards and flyers, explaining the services offered by Carriage Limousine. This was a very successful tool to keep my cars on the streets in plain sight where they could be viewed by prospective clients. Mr. Barsotti and Mr. Joyce were very happy with the services we provided to their customers to give them special evenings.

As time went on, I constantly looked for more new and exciting marketing ideas for my company. I started working with upscale restaurants, promoting them, myself, and other entities. One outstanding package included dinner for two at Ricco's Restaurant in Pittsburgh's North Hills, transportation for the evening provided by Carriage Limousine, and two complimentary round-trip tickets to anywhere in the United States, provided by USAir.

In the photo below, Ricco, the owner of the restaurant, and Sam Szabawsky, my longtime friend who I have mentioned throughout the book, present the Ultimate Prize.

ULTIMATE PRIZE AWARD

I also partnered with the Pittsburgh Pirates and another fine restaurateur, Don DeBlasio of DeBlasio's in Green Tree. This package included dinner for two at DeBlasio's restaurant, all ground transportation provided by Carriage Limousine, and once again, two round-trip tickets to anywhere in the United States, compliments of USAir.

LEFT TO RIGHT, DON DeBLASIO, CARL, JIM LEYLAND

I gained great success with these types of contests, as well as getting a lot of media coverage. All of this helped me to capture a major part the market share.

Along with these two fine dining restaurants, I also worked with Ruth's Chris Steak House in downtown Pittsburgh, owned by the Offenbach family. Jack Offenbach was always open to new marketing ideas that promoted our businesses together.

CHAPTER 5:

SPECIAL DESTINATIONS

I began to explore new and different destinations throughout western Pennsylvania where I could provide upscale transportation services. One of the first places I visited was Seven Springs Mountain Resort in Seven Springs, Pennsylvania. I met with Jim McClure, the chairman of the resort, who introduced me to the director of transportation, who was responsible for transporting people from the Greater Pittsburgh International Airport to the resort. Carriage Limousine became the official transportation company to fulfill their customers' needs.

While working with Seven Springs, I used this opportunity to put dinner packages together marketing Helen's, the fine restaurant on their property. Helen's was the original house of the Dupre family, the founders of Sevens Springs. The resort offered great ski slopes, golf courses, meeting rooms for corporate events, and accommodations. As time went on, I created a great working relationship with Jim McClure.

In the early 1990s, Jim recommended my services to Joe Hardy, who in 1987 purchased a resort that became known as Nemacolin Woodlands Resort. At the meeting with Joe Hardy and his daughter, Maggie, Carriage Limousine was awarded the designation of Nemacolin's transportation company of choice. It was a wonderful and ongoing relationship for many years.

As Nemacolin Woodlands Resort grew, adding many fine restaurants and a world-renowned spa, it gained a five-star resort status. Our business grew with it. Many people flew into the Greater Pittsburgh International Airport who required luxury transportation through the big, beautiful hills of Pennsylvania to the amazing resort. We also fulfilled all the transportation needs for golf tournaments that were held at the prestigious Mystic Rock Golf Course on the property, as well as for corporate meetings, weddings, and special events.

Speaking of destination trips through the mountains of Pennsylvania, we provided many trips during the fall foliage season, visiting historical landmarks including Frank Lloyd Wright's famous home, Fallingwater; Laurel Caverns; the Summit Inn Resort in Farmington; and fine restaurants like Nino's in Mount Pleasant. My clients were always greeted by Nino Barsotti or his daughter, the owners of the restaurant. Nino was the brother of John Barsotti, owner of the famous Common Plea restaurant that I mentioned earlier in the book.

I also marketed a dinner package to the DiSalvo Train Station, a fine restaurant occupying the former Pennsylvania Railroad station in Latrobe, Pennsylvania, operated by Mr. DiSalvo, known as Chef Guy, and his son, Joey. This restaurant had the atmosphere and architecture from the railroad days, making you feel like you were in a unique setting. As you entered through the tunnel to the cobblestone floor, you could enjoy a cocktail at the Tap Room prior to dinner. Going into the restaurant, guests were greeted by Chef Guy and Joey and then escorted to the Prima Classe fine dining car, which has fed many celebrities and VIP guests. It was a dining experience to remember. Guests could have their privacy and enjoy fine Italian dining. The guests were not limited to choosing their meal from a paper menu; guests could make verbal requests, and the chef would prepare anything the client suggested. After dinner, guests would be escorted to one of the finest cigar bars in Westmoreland County, Joey D's.

Joey DiSalvo and I became good friends. I count on Joey to give *everyone* the VIP treatment they deserve. I have personally enjoyed many evenings at this outstanding restaurant with several well-known VIPs. After their visit, many of these special guests would then request my service to transport their guests to the DiSalvo Train Station to enjoy all they had to offer.

Trips to special destinations increased, and relationships with the proprietors grew over the years. The destination revenue source helped grow my limousine business in western Pennsylvania.

I now began to associate my business with all the major sports organizations in Pittsburgh, including the Pittsburgh Penguins, Pittsburgh Steelers, Pittsburgh Pirates, *Pittsburgh Post-Gazette*, and the PGA. I worked with them for major tournaments in Pittsburgh and the surrounding area. I also worked with the three major TV and radio stations in and around Pittsburgh. Later in this book, I will share many stories pertaining to all of the above and some celebrities as well.

I would also be remiss if I didn't again mention Gil Lucas, the founder of the number-one sports cable network in our district. He was better known as "America's Guest." Much of my success came about with his help and his connections in places where I, the owner of a small limousine company, could never have gone. Many doors were opened by his personal referrals. The name of Gil Lucas worked everywhere we went.

CHAPTER 6:

BUSINESS GROWTH WITH LOCAL SPORTS CLIENTELE

THE PITTSBURGH PENGUINS

If you're from Pittsburgh, you understand that if you want your business to be successful and noticed in the marketplace, you must associate yourself and your services with the three major sports teams. I knew my relationship with Gil Lucas could open those doors for me. And once those doors were opened, I took advantage of each one.

My first sports-team client was the Pittsburgh Penguins. In the late 1980s, I was introduced to their owner, Howard Baldwin. Being from Los Angeles, he needed a car every time he was in Pittsburgh. Mr. Baldwin was a fine gentleman, well known from New York to Los Angeles as an American entrepreneur and film producer. His busy schedule kept him in and out of meetings, events, dinners, and so forth, and I assigned one of our drivers, Andy, to be his chauffeur. Mr. Baldwin was so happy and impressed with our service. I asked Andy if I could possibly meet Mr. Baldwin for lunch, and again, I was invited to the prestigious Duquesne Club. I met with him for lunch, and we negotiated. At that lunch, he called his office and advised them to sign us on as the official limousine company of the Pittsburgh Penguins. This would allow us to use the images of the players and the Pens logo on our billboards, in media coverage, and in any of my marketing tools.

One of the services included in the newly signed contract with the Pittsburgh Penguins was to provide transportation as needed to the new players as well as the veterans. Since most new recruits didn't know their way around Pittsburgh, the car was made available for them on call. One of those recruits was Mario Lemieux. I built a great relationship with Mario, and he always remembered we were there for him and his family. Mario was very kind. He never refused to autograph an item for me that I could use to enhance my business. We performed many services for all of the Penguins, but little did we know that Mario Lemieux was going to be such a superstar when we picked him up that first time.

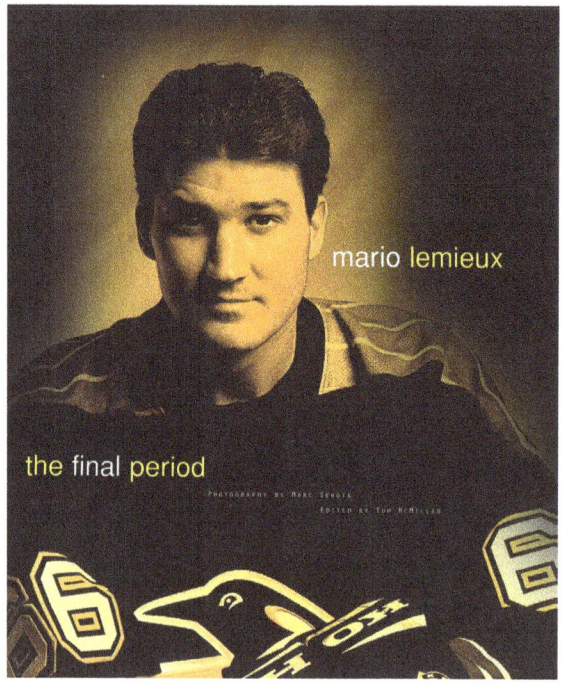

Mario Lemieux

Mario Lemieux, honored as Mr. Pittsburgh

Mario, Carl, Linda, Alain Lemieux

I have a lot of hockey stories. One in particular that comes to mind took place in 1991, when the Penguins won against the Minnesota North Stars for the Stanley Cup. I was on the ground floor of many celebrations that evening, driving through the city with six stretch limousines. With the sunroof open and driving down Penn Avenue, Mario was handing off the Stanley Cup to Jaromir Jagr, limo-to-limo—a sight I will remember forever. We stopped at all the popular night spots, including Chauncey's, Donzi's on the water, the South Side bars, Fox Chapel Yacht Club, and many other Pittsburgh favorites. Team-member players were going in, filling the Cup with champagne, then going on to the next bar.

As we started along Route 28 toward Fox Chapel, the players saw a lot of homes that had been decorated with Penguins signs and flags. In particular, I remember one house had flashing lights, flags, and blown-up hockey players in the yard. The team decided to stop at the house, knock on the door, and ask to use their bathroom. Up to the door they went, and without hesitation, the elderly couple who lived there invited them in! Many of the players accepted the invitation. Carrying the Stanley Cup with them, they offered the couple a drink from it. Photographs were taken with the players and the Stanley Cup. What a sight to see! The neighbors came out of their houses cheering, applauding, and congratulating the team. There were more pictures and autographs with the Cup and the team. It was heartwarming to watch these players giving back to their loyal fans, and it was something those people will remember forever.

After a few more stops, we all proceeded to Mario's house in Upper St. Clair. The house was set up for a party that would never end—catered food, several bars, and a swimming pool. Needless to say, everyone was feeling pretty happy. Someone threw the Stanley Cup into the pool, and as Jaromir pulled it to the surface, the base never came up. So here we were at 1:00 a.m. with the broken Stanley Cup that had to be at the Allegheny County Airport at 5:00 a.m.

Arrangements had been made for the team captain, Bob Errey, to meet the NBC private jet, fly to New York City, and appear on the morning show, displaying the Stanley Cup. Everyone, chauffeurs included, began making calls, searching for a twenty-four-hour service that could spot-weld the Stanley Cup.

The calls sounded something like this: "Hello, this is so-and-so. Can I bring the Stanley Cup by to be welded so I can get it flown New York City early this morning?" After many hang-ups, and several people who did not believe what they were hearing, we realized we had to change this up a little. We began by saying that we had a broken pipe from the water tank that had to be welded. Then we asked if we could bring the pipe to the welder immediately.

Finally, after an hour of making phone calls, more hang-ups, and some name-calling, we reached a registered plumber in Etna. His house and shop were in the same building. He said, "Bring it over, and I'll try to help." We rushed the Cup to his shop. He couldn't believe it when the Stanley Cup that he had seen earlier that evening on television was now on his workbench! He tacked it together as seamlessly as he could, and we were off to the County Airport with it to meet Captain Bob Errey. The Stanley Cup made it to the plane on time, and no one in New York ever knew anything had gone wrong.

If you remember, shortly after this, the National Hockey Association hired a handler for the Stanley Cup. He was well dressed, wearing a black suit and white gloves, with a locked carrying case for which he had the only key. This man was responsible for the safety of Stanley Cup and accompanied it wherever it would go. Every time players would take the Cup somewhere, we transported it in a limo. This was great exposure for Carriage Limousine.

When players' families came to town, I would receive the call to transport them. When players were out partying in the city, they had a special number to call, and we would send two drivers to get the player, and their sports cars, home safely. That way, the next day they had their cars. Jaromir and a couple of other players kept us pretty busy!

Gil Lucas was airing all Penguin hockey games, including playoffs and Stanley Cup games, and made sure I always had a sixty-second commercial during the game. Several of these commercials featured players, including Ron Francis, Troy Loney, Kevin Stevens, and Ulf Samuelson, all using and recommending my services in front of thousands of fans and future customers. I was always questioned how a little limousine company could afford those spots. The answer was always the same: Gil Lucas.

I was invited to many charity golf outings and fundraisers and would donate limousine time and dinners at fine restaurants in the city while proudly displaying the Penguins logo. Also, as I closed my deal with the Pens, I was introduced to Sam Szabawsky, the marketing director of the Pittsburgh Marriott hotel, located across from the Civic Arena. Sam asked if I could arrange a meeting with the Penguins' organization, with the hope that this Marriott could be designated as the official hotel of the Pens. After that meeting, the Pittsburgh Marriot hotel was named the "hotel of choice" for the team and was permitted to use the Pittsburgh Penguins logo.

Sammy and I became the best of friends, and we still are today. He retired in Michigan, and we visit several times a year. That relationship opened many hotel doors for me, including developing an in-town shuttle van service, being the exclusive car service for airport trips and weddings in their ballrooms, and being involved in many other events. Enjoying hotel suites, limos, and VIP tickets to hockey games; playing golf every Monday for charity events; giving back by donating hotel rooms, nights on the town, and fine dining—these things really made us set in the city. Life was good, and friends like Sammy don't come around too often.

Gil Lucas was the renowned and famous world's guest everywhere he went, but he always gave back to his charities and friends—my hero and friend forever.

After the 1991 Stanley Cup games, our phone was ringing off the hook. Weddings, bachelor parties, nights on the town, airport pickups and drop-offs—we were growing at a high rate of speed and buying more equipment. We were the first in the city to have a limo bus that could transport up to sixteen people. It was outfitted with two big-screen TVs, two bars, specialty lighting, a sunroof, and plenty more.

After four months of marketing and advertising this limo bus on my commercials, shown with well-known hockey players stepping out from it, I made a trip to Los Angeles to have two more of these built for us. I can tell you this, with the Pens' back-to-back Stanley Cup wins (winning over the Chicago Blackhawks in 1992), Carriage Limousine was experiencing back-to-back success. I was displaying my limo buses and stretch limos with everyone in the cars—Pens' players, their mascot, and of course, the star of it all, the Stanley Cup.

GOALTENDER TOM BARRASSO'S IN-GAME HOCKEY STICK

GORDIE HOWE IN ACTION

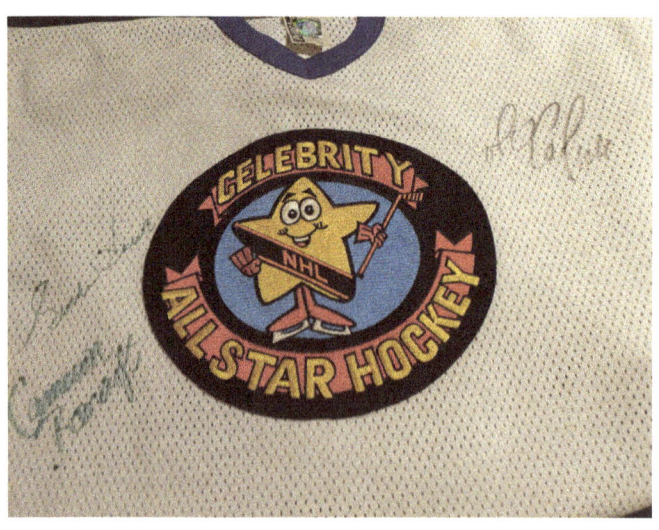

CELEBRITY HOCKEY JERSEY, WITH SIGNATURES OF MARIO LEMIEUX AND GORDIE HOWE ON THIS SAME JERSEY. PRICELESS!

TROY LONEY

ULF SAMUALSON WITH THE STANLEY CUP

SCOTTIE BOWMAN WITH THE STANLEY CUP

KEVIN STEVENS WITH THE STANLEY CUP

You cannot imagine how many brides came to our large garage and reservation center on the South Side to book their wedding limousines. Our waiting room was filled with memorabilia, with each wall dedicated to the people we had driven. One wall featured signed hockey jerseys and autographed hockey sticks and pucks. We had Tom Barrasso's in-game stick from the final games of the 1991 and 1992 Stanley Cup. Both of these sticks were signed by every player, Coach Scotty Bowman, and General Manager Craig Patrick. Another treasure was a 1990 celebrity hockey jersey, with the signatures of Mr. Hockey, Gordie Howe, and our own Mario Lemieux on the same jersey. This jersey and many other autographed memorabilia pieces are among the prized possessions in my man cave today.

BRUCE WILLIS

In late 1992, I had the opportunity to spend some time with Bruce Willis. He was in town filming the popular movie *Striking Distance*. I enjoyed getting to know Bruce. He was a guitar player, bike rider, golfer, and hockey fan, as well as a movie star. As we got to know each other a little better, I asked him if he would like to play golf at my country club, Nevillewood. He said, "I'd love to." As we played the round, I got to learn a lot about *the* Bruce Willis.

This was during the time that the Pittsburgh Penguins played the Chicago Blackhawks in the Stanley Cup playoff game. Bruce asked if I thought I could get a ticket to the game for him. I knew it would almost be impossible, so I called in a favor from the only one person I felt could help me, and the following day, I put a call into Mario Lemieux. If anyone could get tickets for me, it would be Mario. Soon after, Natalie Lemieux called me and told me that there would be two passes available for Bruce and me to sit in the section reserved for the players' wives. The wives were all excited to meet Bruce Willis!

On the night of the game, I sent my driver to the hotel to pick Bruce up. Bruce was out riding his bike. I called him on his cell phone, and he said he would be arriving at the service entrance to the Civic Arena by game time. As the game started, I was sitting in the midst of all the players' wives with an empty seat next to me. I was very nervous as I heard the comments starting, asking, "Where is Bruce?" Up through the first period, there I was, with the empty seat next to me. At the end of the first period, the wives left their seats and went to the private dining area. I was speechless.

Before the start of the second period, a man came in wearing a Penguins cap pulled down over his eyes so no one could see who he was. He sat in the empty seat. When the wives returned, Natalie said to me, "Who is that?" Then Bruce turned around, lifted up his hat and said, "I'm Bruce Willis!" It was a moment to remember.

At the end of the second period, Bruce and I were invited to the join the wives in the private dining area for photos and autographs. The surprise of the evening came when Bruce said to Natalie, "Do you think you could arrange that at the end of the game, I could go down to the Penguins locker room and that I could get an autographed stick from your husband? I'm his biggest fan." Without hesitation, Natalie said, "We can arrange that!" What a thrill it was for me as security walked us into the Penguins' locker room! Mario and Bruce greeted each other and exchanged comments. Mario signed the hat Bruce was wearing and gave him a signed jersey and stick. After Mario gave the signed stick to him, Bruce had several other players sign it as well.

Later that evening, as my driver was taking Bruce, his signed items, and the bike back to the hotel, he wanted to go out for a few drinks. He asked to go to any place that had a jazz group playing. I called Bob, the owner of Mario's on the South Side, and told him I'd like a private table in the back because I was bringing Bruce Willis to the restaurant. Bob said he would give us a secured area where Bruce wouldn't be bothered. As we arrived, with Bruce still wearing the Penguin cap pulled down over his eyes, we entered the secured area. Bruce was enjoying the music.

After a few beers, he asked if he could jam with the group. Bob said he would clear it with the lead guitarist. His comment was. "Bruce Willis! Bring him on stage!" As Bruce approached the stage, the lead guitarist had made the announcement, "We have a celebrity in the house tonight who is going to jam with us. Please allow me to introduce Bruce Willis." Bruce was like a little kid in a candy store, jamming with the group until closing time, taking photos and signing autographs. For me, it was another night to remember.

THE PITTSBURGH PIRATES BASEBALL CLUB

WILLIE STARGELL

WILLIE STARGELL AND TERRY BRADSHAW

WILLIE STARGELL, CARL AND GUEST

1994 All-Star Game program

Willie Stargell's signed hat

MEAT LOAF'S SIGNED HAT

The third wall highlighted the Pittsburgh Pirates. Hats, baseballs, programs, and shirts were all signed by some of the great players, like Willie Stargell, Steve Blass, Jim Rooker, Dick Groat, Bill Mazeroski, and Roy Face. There were many more baseballs signed by all the players. From Jim Leyland, there were pictures and special programs from the 1994 All-Star Game and the hats worn by Hall of Famer Willie Stargell. Recording artist Meat Loaf signed a hat for me, as well as the game ball.

After the All-Star Game, Willie wanted to go to a restaurant in Pittsburgh's Hill District, where free chicken wings were handed out every time Willie hit a home run, which was often! I informed Willie, known as Pops, that there had been a lot of changes, and the Hill wasn't like it used to be; it wasn't the safe environment it had been before. But Willie insisted, and how could I say no to him? We arranged a police escort, added more security, and made the trip to the restaurant. Upon entering, everyone inside gave Willie a standing ovation. Willie yelled out, "Chicken wings for all!" We stayed around, and Willie was signing autographs, shaking hands, answering questions, and remembering good times. This is another memory that I'll never forget; it was the last time I would see Willie.

Some of the most enjoyable times that I've spent with the baseball greats took place after the games, when Steve Blass, Jim Rooker, Dick Groat, Myron Cope, Gil Lucas, and Bill Hillgrove would go out drinking and partying. They always traveled in a Carriage Limousine, and we made sure that everyone got home safely. I played a lot of golf with this group too. I visited them when they were in Bradenton, Florida, at the Pirate training camp. We enjoyed several rounds of golf at Champion Lakes, which was owned by Jerry Lynch and Dick Groat.

I always had an open invitation to join Bill Mazeroski at his golf course, located in his hometown of Hempfield, Pennsylvania. When Bill was a boy, he was not allowed to cut across this course to go fishing—now he owns it! We packed up my limo bus, filled it with beer and a whiskey of their choice, and traveled from Conneaut Lake, where Hillgrove had a cabin that slept eight people—that's two foursomes! We had many good times, joking, laughing, drinking, and telling stories that I can't repeat in this book.

Bill Hillgrove was well known as the voice of the Pittsburgh Steelers and Pitt basketball, with Dick Groat and Don DeBlasio as his spotters. Since we were friends, I asked him to be the voice of Carriage Limousine. Immediately, he answered yes. From then on, when a caller was put on hold, they would hear Bill Hillgrove's voice promoting my business and talking about our services. Carriage Limousine couldn't have had a better spokesperson.

THE PITTSBURGH STEELERS

2005 PITTSBURGH STEELERS
First Row: Jeff Reed, Ben Roethlisberger, Tommy Maddox, Quincy Morgan, Charlie Batch, Chris Gardocki, Bryant McFadden, Ricardo Colclough, Duce Staley, Tyrone Carter, Ike Taylor, Deshea Townsend, Willie Williams.
Second Row: Chris Hope, Chidi Iwuoma, Mike Logan, Verron Haynes, Dan Kreider, Jerome Bettis, Bill Cowher, Noah Herron, Willie Parker, Troy Polamalu, Larry Foote, James Farrior, Clark Haggans.
Third Row: Dick Hoak, Ken Whisenhunt, Rian Wallace, Joey Porter, Chukky Okobi, Clint Kriewaldt, Greg Warren, Jeff Hartings, Alan Faneca, Kimo von Oelhoffen, Chris Kemoeatu, Barrett Brooks, Kendall Simmons, Dick LeBeau, Ariko Iso.
Fourth Row: James Daniel, Mark Whipple, Chris Hoke, Marvel Smith, Max Starks, Trai Essex, Cedrick Wilson, Sean Morey, Antwaan Randle El, Heath Miller, Jerame Tuman, Darren Perry, Ray Horton.
Fifth Row: Russ Grimm, Bruce Arians, Nate Washington, Hines Ward, Matt Kranchick, Travis Kirschke, Aaron Smith, James Harrison, Casey Hampton, Brett Keisel, John Mitchell, Keith Butler.
Sixth Row: Kevin Spencer, Matt Raich, Kalvin Jones, Rich Baker, Rodgers Freyvogel, Rob Brakel, Bob McCartney, Andy Lizanich, John Norwig, Ryan Grove, Ray Jackson, Marcel Pastoor, Lou Spanos, Chet Fuhrman.

SUPER PITTSBURGH STEELERS

One of our other walls featured Pittsburgh Steelers footballs, jerseys, and other items, all signed by the greats, including Franco Harris, Terry Bradshaw, Rocky Bleier, Jerome Bettis, Mel Blount, and Hines Ward. The memorabilia includes a football signed by Coach Bill Cowher, and even "Big Ben" Roethlisberger's hat, jerseys, and other items.

When I offered a proposal to the Steelers' management for Carriage Limousine to be the official transportation company for the team, I received a lot of pushback from the owners. Art Rooney Sr. was not very interested. After several meetings with his son, Dan, and with the help of my good friend Gil Lucas, we began providing some of their ground transportation needs. After working with the Steelers for several months, we earned the right to become the official transportation company for our Pittsburgh Steelers.

Of course, there were different requests as to how we handle the business with them. We were always the recommended company to use, but when players personally used the services, it was on them. When reservations were made by the front office of the Steelers, they would pick up the tab. It was also made clear by management that only black cars or dark-colored stretch limousines were to be used for four or more passengers. For example, these vehicles were used to pick passengers up at the airport who were brought into town for a meeting, to shuttle them around the city, or for bringing draft picks to the new sports complex on the South Side of Pittsburgh.

Because Carriage Limousine always provided the Steelers with service that included on-time pickup, professional chauffeurs, and clean cars, we earned the right to do more business with them. The front office recommended us to their professional contacts, and we also enjoyed many personal requests from the players, especially when their families came into town. Visiting AFL and NFL teams, owners, and upper management also used our services to and from the game.

JEROME BETTIS

In 1993, a new player was one of the first to be picked up at the airport. His name was Jerome Bettis, chosen in the 1993 draft. We were told to stay with him, driving him to the hotel and then off to dinner at Morton's The Steak House. The following morning, we were to drive him to the Steelers' office.

Surprisingly enough, I was enjoying a cocktail at Morton's bar, which I frequented because they always had a good happy hour, when Jerome arrived at the restaurant. I introduced myself as the owner of the car service that had picked him up and welcomed him to Pittsburgh, and I told him that we would be driving him while he was in town. Jerome and I struck up some conversation, and I gave my personal business card to him, telling him that he should call me directly for anything he needed and that I would handle it personally. Our personal relationship began on that day, and after twenty-eight years, I still consider him a friend.

There are many great Jerome Bettis stories out there. He was an outstanding player who had a super personality. While Jerome's popularity grew, Carriage Limousine was growing, and our personal relationship grew as well. The need for the services we offered became more important to him. As busy as he became with demands for personal appearances, he would always show up in a Carriage Limousine, including to the weekly *Jerome Bettis Show* and many different events.

Jerome asked if he could be assigned only one particular chauffeur, Larry. I explained that we normally didn't do that for many different reasons. But after further discussions with Jerome, how could I say no? Shortly after that request, Larry became Jerome's personal concierge, driving "the bus" wherever he requested and traveling from state to state. Larry thanked me many times for giving him that opportunity and for all the things that would lie ahead for him. We'll save that for another story.

For the weekly *Jerome Bettis Show*, we would pick up his guests in a stretch limousine, stocked with the beverage of their choice. The show quickly picked up steam. With a live audience and popular football players answering questions at random, it was good TV.

PITTSBURGH STEELERS JACKET SIGNED BY KORDELL STEWART

After the show, it was party time, and we had some great ones. In particular, I remember the time he invited our quarterback, Kordell Stewart, to be a guest. Most people knew that Kordell wasn't a fan favorite. He never signed autographs and didn't interview well. It was as if he thought he was the *greatest*, and that didn't make him popular with Pittsburgh fans.

My friend Sam was with me that night and bet me that Kordell would not sign anything for me. Of course, I had to prove that he was wrong. As the show ended, Kordell headed to the limo that was waiting for him and Jerome so they could party. As we waited, I got in the car and introduced myself as the owner of the company, and I asked Kordell for his autograph for my wall of fame. He respectfully stated, "I don't sign," so I then explained how this was going to work. "This car with Larry driving picked you up, brought you here, and now is going to take you out to party. Well, that isn't going to happen, and you will need to find another way back to North Hills because I'll give Larry his instructions."

Very surprised, and I think shocked that this was happening to the great Kordell, he immediately said, "I don't even carry a Sharpie!" I reached into my pocket and handed him a brand-new one, and I asked him to sign the back of my leather Steelers jacket right in the center of the white part of the logo! It is another one of my prized possessions.

Shortly after that, Jerome and my friend Sam got into the car, and this subject was never mentioned again. We partied until the wee hours of the morning, then dropped everyone safely at their homes. From that day forward, I had a good relationship with Kordell. He, as well as his family, used my services.

Another thing about Jerome was that he was always available for me to autograph footballs and jerseys, and sometimes for personal appearances. We played a little golf together and had many good times. He never forgot who the first person to welcome him to Pittsburgh was.

Hines Ward

Working with the Pittsburgh Steelers' front office and players, I created some fine long-term relationships. This is one of the great ones.

Hines Ward was one of my favorite players. He hired our service for many of his personal events, and this one was the biggest of them all. I informed my staff that on Friday morning, we had a special guest coming to make some arrangements for his upcoming wedding. I told them this was going to be a big one, and his name was Hines Ward. Everyone was so excited. Even the girls who had the day off showed up!

Hines and his fiancée, Simone, came in Friday morning as promised with Dunkin' Donuts in hand. I greeted them and introduced them to my office staff. Everyone in the office was star struck. After everyone settled down, I gave Hines and Simone a tour of our facility, and then Gail, my personal assistant, helped to lay out transportation plans for their wedding, bachelor and bachelorette parties, shuttles from the airport for out-of-town guests, and back-and-forth transportation to their hotels. They requested that everyone be driven in stretch limos, stocked with bottles of champagne and several other beverages. The bride and groom would be riding in my classic white Rolls-Royce, Silver Spur model, as the lead car.

After all of their arrangements had been made and contact information had been exchanged, Hines stayed behind to take photographs and to sign jerseys, footballs, and other items. Then my surprise came—Hines invited my wife and me to attend their wedding. Honored and very excited, we accepted. We had a great time rubbing elbows with all the Steelers, Coach Cowher, and the Rooney family. The entire team was there. It was a wedding I will never forget.

When they returned from their honeymoon, Hines invited me for a round of golf. He wanted to thank my staff and me for such good service and for making that special day perfect for him, Simone, and all of their guests.

He and his new wife were receiving great responses from everyone we had transported. They were asking for our name and contact information. Of course, I supplied him with a lot of my personal business cards. He also wanted to be sure that everyone on the Steelers' team had one of my cards. Anytime he could, Hines Ward would personally recommend my services. That advertising was priceless; I would never have been able to afford that commercial!

Thanks to Hines, I saw a lot of Steelers' football games from a private box. We became good friends. Anytime I needed to call on him, he was always available. This leads to some other limo stories that I will share with you later in my book.

FOOTBALL GREATS
"BROADWAY" JOE NAMATH

JOE NAMATH AND THE EXCALIBUR

"Broadway" Joe Namath was born and raised in Beaver Falls, Pennsylvania. When Joe would come into the city, we always transported him back and forth to the airport and to any special events. I had the opportunity to play a round of golf at a charity golf outing at Southpointe, in Canonsburg, Pennsylvania, where Joe was guest of honor. Joe helped me to promote my business, and I donated limousine service and dinner for four at Southpointe, and an autographed football from Joe Namath. Joe had photos taken with my newly designed Excalibur.

Joe and I created a relationship where Carriage Limousine would be of service to his elderly parents, still living in Beaver Falls. He gave us the number of his gold American Express Card, and told us to use this to perform any kind of service his parents may need, including their trips to and from the airport, since they frequently visited Joe at his home in Florida.

TONY DORSETT

TONY DORSETT'S SIGNED PITT UNIVERSITY HAT

Another great Hall of Famer, Tony Dorsett, originally from Aliquippa, Pennsylvania, always used my limousine service.

I remember one particular time when I asked him for an autographed photo. He said, "I'll do one better," and he gave me one of his Pitt ball caps, signed "HOF."

He was always a fine gentleman with whom to do business. He even visited our company headquarters, taking pictures and signing autographs for the staff.

CHAPTER 7:
THE GREATS OF GOLF

The walls of my personal office were filled with something that is near and dear to me: my collection of golf memorabilia. I was hired by Rolex, in conjunction with the PGA, for the 1994 US Open as their official transportation company. This happened before car companies supplied them with new luxury cars.

PHIL MICKELSON'S BAG AND CARL

JACK NICKLAUS'S SIGNED VISOR FROM THE INAUGURAL ROUND AT NEVILLEWOOD GOLF CLUB

One of first people we were to pick up was a twenty-four-year-old golfer whom Rolex was grooming to be a superstar. They were right; that young golfer was Phil Mickelson. They employed us to have a car staged eighteen hours a day for Phil and his family to use. This started a friendship between us that went on for many years. Besides Phil Mickelson, I enjoyed meeting Jack Nicklaus, Tom Watson, and of course, Arnold Palmer.

ARNOLD PALMER'S SIGNED HAT, WORN IN THE 1994 US OPEN

1994 MARCH OF DIMES GOLF CLASSIC
OAKMONT COUNTRY CLUB
U.S. OPEN

ARNOLD PALMER AND ROCCO MEDIATE

Being selected as the company of choice for the 1994 US Open, we ran ninety pieces of equipment, which consisted of sedans, stretch limousines, shuttle vans, and helicopters to transport Arnold Palmer and Winnie, his wife. This was to be the last major tournament in which he would participate. We had been doing business with Arnie for several years when he was living in Latrobe; Carriage Limousine was his car company of choice.

On Friday at Oakmont Country Club, coming up to the eighteenth hole with tears running down his face, Arnold Palmer said goodbye to his many fans. What a moment to remember! His many fans, knowing this would be the final hole and last major tournament for Arnie, wanted him to know how much he had done to make golf what it is today. After a press conference, autograph session, and big farewell dinner, we were supposed to bring a chopper in to take him and his wife back to Latrobe. However, due to fog conditions, the plans were changed, and we brought a stretch limousine to transport the Palmers.

Knowing when they were to depart, I made my way to the caddy shed and lifted the flag off the stick from Arnold Palmer's final hole. As Arnie and Winnie were leaving the club and about to enter the limo, I asked Arnie to sign the flag. I'll never forget his words: "Carl, where did you get that?" My answer was that it was to be a souvenir to hang in my office. I handed him a Sharpie, and he signed it. I had this flag professionally framed and hung it on my office wall for several years.

ARNOLD PALMER; MY MOTHER, PEARL; CARL

MY MOTHER, PEARL, STANDING NEXT TO ONE OF OUR HELICOPTERS

A Dream That Came True

As time went on, at eighty-eight years old, my mother learned that Arnold Palmer's birthday was within two days of her birthday. She said to me, "You know, Carl, I never met Arnold Palmer." Immediately, I thought the most perfect birthday gift for my mother was to make it happen and have my mother give Arnold Palmer a birthday present. What a plan!

I knew Doc, Arnie's personal agent, so I called him, asking if I could bring my mother to Latrobe to meet *the King*. Doc said he would check the schedule and call me back. Shortly after, Doc called and told me, "Arnie would love to meet your mom."

I wrapped up the framed flag and told my mother we were going out to lunch. I had a limousine pick her up at the nursing home, and we were driven to the Palmers' home in Latrobe, Pennsylvania. When we arrived, my mother couldn't believe what was happening; she was overwhelmed when I told her that she was going to meet Arnie Palmer. Doc met us as we arrived and walked with us into Arnie's personal office. Arnie, who was seated behind his desk, got up and greeted us. A table was prepared for a lunch with the King.

As we finished our lunch, Mom said, "Mr. Palmer, this is from me and my son. We've brought you a very special birthday present." Shocked as he was, he said, "That's not necessary," and he unwrapped the gift. Remembering what that flag meant to him, he was so happy and appreciative. I saw that he was emotional when a tear dropped from his eye. He then immediately called Doc and asked that he bring one of the photographers into the room to take some photos. Arnie promised that after the photos were developed, he would sign them and send them to us. With that, he told my mother he was honored to meet her and said some very nice things about me. She couldn't wait to share this story with all the residents at the nursing home! I could not have given her a better present for her eighty-eighth birthday.

My former office, now my man cave, is filled with all the autographed hats and golf balls from many golfers, including Arnold Palmer, Jack Nicklaus, Tom Watson, Gary Player, Lee Trevino, Ernie Ells, Vijay Singh, Fred Couples, and many more. I have hats signed by

Tiger Woods and the world's number-one golfer, Rory McIlroy. I have a priceless collection of autographs and memories from events when and where I interacted with many of my heroes. I also have memorabilia from many PGA tournaments at Hilton Head; the Heritage; Jack's home, the Memorial in Columbus, Ohio; Laurel Valley; and the Senior Tour at Fox Chapel Golf Club. I've spent time with Kenny Perry and Tom Watson during priceless moments after working with PGA Association. I was always given VIP tickets to high-profile events and enjoyed many of these "inside the ropes" moments during the practice rounds.

Of all my memorabilia, the signed photograph with Arnold Palmer; my mother, Pearl; the flag from the eighteenth hole of the 1994 US Open at Oakmont; and me is my most prized possession.

MASTERS CHAMPS

CHAPTER 8:
CELEBRITIES

I also have a wall featuring photos and memorabilia from the celebrities I have met, from Michael Jackson to the Rat Pack of the 1980s, Charlton Heston, and many other names I'm sure you'll recognize. I hope you enjoy their stories.

INTRODUCTION

As we grew and earned the reputation in Pittsburgh as the number-one transportation company, the phone was ringing off the hook. We were becoming well known nationwide, and we were driving for celebrities and out-of-town sports teams. It was an exciting time in my life. Many agencies would make reservations with us for out-of-town guests, movie companies, and movie stars. If you remember, back in the 1990s, a lot of movies were being made in Pittsburgh. I will now share with you some of my personal experiences of meeting some of the most famous people in the world.

CARL J. GASPER, JR.

CHARLTON HESTON

CHARLTON HESTON

AUTOGRAPHED PHOTO FROM CHARLTON HESTON

CHARLTON HESTON

April 17, 1997

Dear Mr. Gasper:

    First I want to thank you for the professional care you gave me during my time in Pittsburgh; I appreciate anyone who does his job with planning and accuracy. You did that and more.

    Please accept the enclosed photographs for your mother and for your office with my best wishes and all good luck now and in the future.

Cordially,

THE LETTER I RECEIVED FROM CHARLTON HESTON

Charlton Heston was one of my favorites. Our company got a call from Sister Mary Ellen, the director of the Little Sisters of the Poor. They had invited Charlton Heston to be the main speaker at a charity event to be held at the DoubleTree hotel. As the trips were called into us, my assistant informed me for whom we would be driving. I immediately said, "I'll drive this one."

The next day, I put on my chauffer attire and had Shawn shine up the car, stocking it with the local newspaper and many beverages. I was on my way to pick up Sister Mary Ellen, and we would then proceed to the Allegheny County Airport to meet the private jet that was soon to arrive. As the jet landed, we pulled up to the tarmac, and *the* Charlton Heston got off the plane, along with his manager and security guard. They were greeted by Sister Mary Ellen and proceeded to the car, where I was standing and ready to open the door.

I said, "Mr. Heston, welcome to Pittsburgh." He answered me back with that strong, deep voice: "You can call me Chuck."

As I was driving to the hotel, looking in the rearview mirror, I realized this was Charlton Heston in the rear seat, facing forward! I was listening to that well-recognized deep voice, the one I remembered from movies like *Ben-Hur*, *The Ten Commandments*, *Moses*, and many other great ones. Here I was, driving one of my favorite movie stars—what an unbelievable experience!

As we arrived at the hotel, "Chuck" exited the car and said, "Nice ride," and thanked me. I responded, "Enjoy your stay." Before departing, his manager stepped up and said, "Mr. Heston needs to be picked up tomorrow morning at 5:00 a.m., and he would prefer you to drive." Obviously, I said, "I'll be there."

The next day, I was at my office bright and early. My staff had a stretch limo shined up, stocked with coffee, juices, doughnuts, and the morning newspaper. I was off to the hotel, ready and waiting for my passengers. The manager and security guard brought their luggage out and got into the car. Shortly after that, Chuck came out. As I opened the back door, I greeted him with a "Good morning." His response to me was, "I'll be riding up front with you." I said, "You should sit in the back; I have your coffee ready." He said, "I still would prefer to be up front with you." (Wow!)

As we began our ride to the airport, the conversation started. Chuck said, "Carl, how long have you owned the company, and how many cars in your fleet?" My first response was, "How did you know that I was the owner?" Chuck explained, "You know, my people are aware of everyone we do business with for my safety."

So here we, are driving to the airport and just chatting away. I said, "Normally, one of my chauffeurs would be driving you, but when the call came in, I wanted to have the opportunity to meet you." I proceeded to tell him that my mother was one of his biggest fans and asked if he would send a signed photo to her. He said, "Sure, what's her name?" Then he said, "Are you fan, and would you like me to send you one as well?" We both laughed, and I said, "I have a special place in my office to display it!"

As the conversation went on, he said he was on his way to Los Angeles to meet his grandson Jack Heston. They were meeting with the publishing company.

I can tell you, I never wanted that trip to end. As we pulled up to the jet, he thanked me for my services and stated, "When any of my peers come to Pittsburgh, I'll tell them to look you up. Nice clean cars; on-time, professional service." He also said, "When I get back to my desk, I will get the photographs out to you and your mother."

Within the same week, I received an overnight package from Chuck's office with signed photos—one for Pearl, my mother; one for me personally; one for the wall in my office—and a personally signed letter. I include a copy of that letter in this book.

GREGORY PECK

GREGORY PECK

Another great story took place, thanks to my new friend Charlton Heston.

I was sitting in my office a couple weeks after meeting Charlton Heston when a phone call came from a man asking to speak directly to me. My secretary said, "Carl, Gregory Peck is on the line and will only speak to you." I said "Who's fooling around now?" I told her to put the call through. Believing that someone was playing games, I answered the call in a smart-ass way. It went like something like this: "Hey, Gregory, how in the hell are you? I haven't heard from you in a while."

A voice from the other end of the phone asked, in a very hesitant manner, "Is this the Carl Gasper who owns Carriage Limousine Company?" He continued, "I was talking to my good friend Charlton Heston. When I told him I have a week's appearance at The Pittsburgh Public Theater in Pittsburgh, Pennsylvania, he immediately told me that I should call his friend Carl Gasper, who will take care of all of mine and my wife's transportation needs." At that point, I realized it really *was* Gregory Peck on the other end of the line! I apologized over and over again and explained to him I receive several crank calls every day, and sometimes my buddies would play jokes on me. Gregory went on to say that Chuck was very impressed with my service, and told him to use his name. Chuck had told him, "Carl will make sure you will be well taken care of."

We then took care of the reservation. Gregory wanted a car to be on call ten hours a day for the duration of his stay. With a car at her disposal, his wife could visit the popular Pittsburgh attractions, as he was busy working and rehearsing daily for the big show. I assigned my number-one chauffer, Andy, who was born and raised in the city. He knew all the sights very well.

During his stay, Gregory Peck invited my wife and me to join them for dinner. I made reservations at Monterey Bay so they could enjoy the view of our beautiful city.

After his final performance, the theater held a grand, fancy going-away party, to which my wife and I were invited guests. We were seated at the table with Gregory and his wife. What an honor and experience! It was a night to remember.

The following day, I personally drove the couple to the airport (no charge for that one). I thanked him for the business and told him, "If you talk to Chuck, thank him for the referral, and tell him to call me so we can discuss his referral fee!" We both had a good laugh. As I dropped them off at the airport, he said, "Now you have two people in Hollywood promoting your business. Good luck and God bless."

MICHAEL JACKSON

Michael Jackson was one of the biggest stars we ever drove, and I'd like to share some of his most unusual transportation needs.

In September of 1988, we received a call from Michael's agent in LA to arrange transportation for Michael, his crew, his security detail, and his management staff. This was a big one! As soon as the media announced his show date at the Pittsburgh Civic Arena, the fans were excited and would be monitoring his every move, starting with him arriving on his 747 at Corporate Jets, adjacent to the Greater Pittsburgh International Airport.

On the day of his arrival, all local TV stations, the *Pittsburgh Post-Gazette*, and many reporters were there. We dispatched four black stretch limousines, one van, and four dark-windowed sedans for security detail. With a police escort, we drove the Parkway to the DoubleTree hotel in Pittsburgh. As we pulled up to the main entrance, there were hundreds of fans waiting just to get a glimpse of Michael. My understanding from the GM was that Michael had rented the top floor of the hotel weeks ahead of time, taking out walls to make a larger room so he and his performers could practice and train there, getting ready for the big night.

That afternoon, the GM of the hotel, Joe Kane, and I got together to finalize their service needs. Over our lunch, Joe said to me, "Carl, you don't know, do you?" I asked, "Know what?" Joe continued, "Last week, when I sent a couple of Lincoln Town Cars and one stretch limousine to the airport, is when some of Michael's team arrived. Also, Michael arrived in a custom-made van, with seating for two armed security guards and a built-in cage because he travels with his ape. They arrived and entered through the underground service entrance."

I said, "Joe, that can't be. I just met him at the airport."

Joe continued, "For his personal safety and security, Michael travels with a look-alike everywhere he goes. That's who you picked up. That's who you will be driving around by the direction of Michael's agent. Michael has been in town for over a week. He travels with his own chef and waitstaff. Michael never comes out. Michael only travels in his custom paneled van and his own private jet. The only person who knows when he arrives and when he departs is his agent."

I said, "Amazing! I just can't believe it."

Joe arranged for me to meet the real Michael Jackson, who said he was informed that we were doing a good job, and he appreciated the professional service we were providing, along with the privacy to keep him safe.

What an experience! On the night of the show, we had four front-row seats. It was a spectacular performance. As directed, we were driving the look-alike around. As he left his hotel on his way to the Civic Arena, he slightly opened the darkened windows, waving to the fans with the traditional white glove. At the end of the show, the agent informed me that as the last song was playing, and a large puff of smoke filled the arena, at that time the switch would be made. That's when Michael's look-alike was let down from the roof of the arena, lip-syncing. Everyone was applauding, screaming, and shouting out, "More, more, and more!" Little did they know Michael was already in his van with his ape and his private security guards, heading toward Corporate Jets to get on his giant Boeing 747 plane. He was waiting on the plane for our arrival so he and his team could continue on their way back to Los Angeles.

When the show ended, we exited from underneath the arena, with Michael's look-alike putting down the window and waving his white glove. What a sight! There were several limos, a police escort, and fans following behind, heading to the Greater Pittsburgh International Airport to arrive at the Corporate Jets hub.

As we entered the gated area, there it was—the giant Boeing 747 with Michael's picture on the tail of the plane! It was definitely the biggest plane I have ever seen. This was right up there as one the stories that I wanted to share with you.

THE RAT PACK

Frank Sinatra, Dean Martin, Sammy Davis Jr.

In March of 1988, the office got a phone call from New York City, regarding Sammy Davis Jr., Dean Martin, and Frank Sinatra, well known as the Rat Pack. They were coming to Pittsburgh to perform at the Civic Arena and staying at the downtown Marriott, which was located across the street from the venue.

The first two pickups at the Allegheny County Airport were for Dean Martin and Sammy Davis Jr., arriving the day before the event on the same private jet. On the day of the event, Frank Sinatra and his wife, Barbara, arrived. They had two jets; Frank and Barbara were on one plane, his manager and a security detail on the other. I personally was there to welcome them to Pittsburgh.

Before Frank and his wife exited the plane, I was introduced to the head of security. I was given instructions detailing how we would travel to the city. There were four black Lincoln sedans with darkened windows and a matching stretch limousine, which was used as the decoy car. The head of security informed me that his people would be driving the cars; my drivers were permitted to ride along but not do the actual driving. Frank's people were to be in total control. I said, "They're not insured." He immediately handed me a multimillion-dollar insurance policy to protect their concerns.

As Barbara and Frank exited the plane, they directed one of the Town Cars to the pad. I greeted them both, welcomed them to Pittsburgh, and informed them that I would be riding up front in the passenger seat. Frank said to me, "That's fine."

As we exited the airport, the normal route was set. Coming through Hazelwood, one stretch limo and two Town Cars followed the standard route to the Marriott. The car carrying Frank, Barbara, and me took a completely different route. We were followed by another of the black Town Cars. I later learned that the other car carried Frank's security detail. The first cars to arrive at the Marriott were greeted by several fans, but Frank and Barbara were nowhere to be seen. Our car arrived at the Marriott through the attached parking garage, and Frank and Barbara, along with their security people, entered through the service entrance.

Later that evening, we transported everyone by stretch limousine across the Boulevard, going underneath the Civic Arena. My friend Sam, the general manager of the Marriott, and I, along with our guests, had front-row seating for the show, as well as backstage passes for after the show. Everyone with backstage passes was able to enjoy photo ops and autograph signings.

After the show, transportation back to the hotel had been arranged for all three stars. However, much to my surprise, Frank and his detail drove directly to the Allegheny County Airport to meet his private jets and return home to New York.

Dean Martin and Sammy Davis Jr. elected to stay in Pittsburgh to enjoy some of the sights of the city. After a couple of days in Pittsburgh, Sammy Davis Jr., arranged a lunch for himself and me. At that lunch, he told me that he appreciated our professional service and commented on how he really had enjoyed his visit. He also told me that if he returned to Pittsburgh, he would certainly use our services. He gave me a personally signed photo for my office wall of fame that I have to this day.

The following day, Dean ordered a Lincoln Town Car to take him back to his roots in Steubenville, Ohio. Dean was born there on June 7, 1917, as Dino Paul Crocetti. We found that the street now had a gazebo and historical marker at Route 7 and North Fourth Street, where it was rededicated (in 1996) as Dean Martin Boulevard. He stopped at his childhood home, knocked on the door, and asked if he could visit the home where he was born and raised. The current homeowners were more than happy to let him revisit his former home. He also stopped by Grant Elementary and Steubenville High School, remembering where he originally started as a singer.

When he returned from visiting his old stomping grounds, I said to him, "I couldn't help but notice that you've brought along your golf clubs. Would you be interested in playing one of the finest golf clubs in the world, Oakmont Country Club?" Oakmont Country Club was designated in 1987 as a historical landmark. Of course, he said he was interested! I was able to make some phone calls that would make it happen. I called a good friend of mine, Bob Ford, the pro at the club. He had informed me that he could arrange for us to play on Monday. Monday is normally reserved as a day for special events and is not open to the membership. We agreed that there could be a limited number of fans present that day, and Bob Ford took care of the details.

The following Monday, I had a limo pick up Dean and me and drive us to Oakmont Country Club. We were greeted by Bob Ford and one of the members, who would complete our foursome for the round of golf. Being a member at Bellaire Country Club and carrying a six handicap, Dean was up for the challenge. I was carrying a nine handicap at Hillcrest Country Club in Pittsburgh, and must admit that I was a nervous wreck. We won't be discussing scores here, but we did enjoy a great round of golf, many laughs, and a few cocktails at the end of the round. As we departed the country club, Dean graciously took a lot of photos with the VIP guests, signed a lot of autographs, and said he really enjoyed the course and that it was one of the finest courses he had ever played.

Before he left Pittsburgh, Dean gave me the phone number for his agent. Later, during a personal trip to Las Vegas to see Dean Martin's show at The Sands hotel, I was able to again meet with Dean. He invited me to join him as a part of a foursome and play a round of golf at the Desert Inn, which was one of his favorite courses in Las Vegas. What a day to remember! We talked about his Pittsburgh visit, his trip back to Steubenville, and the Oakmont Country Club round of golf.

Who knew that 1988 was going to be such a banner year for Carriage Limousine—the Rat Pack in March and Michael Jackson in September!

In the early 1990s, while enjoying the growth and the popularity of my company, I continued to solicit more business.

Carl J. Gasper, Jr.

Tris Imboden Bill Champlin Jason Scheff Walt Parazaider Lee Loughnane Robert Lamm Jimmy Pankow Dawayne Bailey

Chicago

Freddie Jackson

LITTLE ANTHONY

BRIAN JAMES

ELVIRA

I had an opportunity to meet Pittsburgh's well renowned Porky Chedwick, "the Platter Pushin' Papa," and also Rich Engler from DiCesare-Engler Productions. These two gentlemen were known for booking many singers and vocal groups to appear at different locations in Pittsburgh, including the Civic Arena. Understanding that many celebrities, singers and musicians would need VIP ground transportation, I struck a deal with these gentlemen, making Carriage Limousine the service that they would call for their ground transportation needs. Some of the groups we transported included the Pointer Sisters, Chicago, Freddie Jackson, Little Anthony and the Imperials, Brian James, Al Martino, Stevie Wonder, Ray Charles, the Vogues, Jamie Foxx, Bobby Vinton, the Dramatics and many more. Allow me to share a few of the stores that I remember.

STEVIE WONDER

Stevie Wonder came to the city to perform in the Strip District. We were requested to provide VIP ground transportation from the airport to the hotel, to the event, and finally, back to the Greater Pittsburgh International Airport. I sent two beautiful white limousines on the evening of the event.

My wife and I had VIP passes for front-row seats and backstage passes to meet Stevie Wonder. It was a phenomenal show, completely sold out. After meeting Stevie backstage and having him autograph photos for my wall of fame, we exited through the back door, where our two white stretch limousines were waiting to transport him to the airport.

With fans all around us, Stevie addressed me and said, "My favorite color, black stretch limousines." The crowd was dead silent. Then Stevie said, "I knew they were white all the time!" We all laughed and applauded as we saw him off on his way to the airport.

RICHARD SIMMONS

RICHARD SIMMONS

Richard Simmons came to Pittsburgh in 1994 from his home located in the French Quarter of New Orleans. He would be performing his exercise and dance routine at the Century 3 Mall.

I went to the airport to meet him. As his security guards questioned me as to who I was, Richard, wearing his traveling shorts, ran at me and jumped into my arms, saying, "Take me to the dance." Stunned and taken aback, for once, I was at a loss for words. It was the beginning of a long-term relationship. From that time forward, we were on call for two days, taking him to his many interviews and appearances through the city. Richard revisited Pittsburgh many times in the 1990s, being brought in by UPMC and Mellon Bank to promote exercise and good health habits. He would always call me personally to arrange his transportation needs while he was in town. Many times, he invited me to come to New Orleans to visit him. This is one example of many relationships that were formed with high-profile celebrities, simply because we provided good-quality professional services.

PHYLLIS DILLER

TIM CONWAY

A couple of the comedians we drove for were Phyllis Diller and Tim Conway. Just thinking about them, the tears of laughter are rolling down my face. They were just as funny in person as they were during a performance.

TIM CONWAY

In 1989, I had the pleasure of providing ground transportation for Tim Conway. I was also given the opportunity for my wife and me to have dinner with Tim, some of his staff, and Harvey Korman. If Carol Burnett would have shown up, we would have thought we were on the television show! It was a night of laughter, jokes, and storytelling that was priceless. The following day, we were invited to his performance. Being treated as VIPs was very rewarding.

JEAN-CLAUDE VAN DAMME

JEAN-CLAUDE VAN DAMME'S HAT WORN DURING THE FILMING OF SUDDEN DEATH

In 1995, when Howard Baldwin, owner of the Pittsburgh Penguins Production Company, filmed a movie at the Civic Arena called *Sudden Death*, the lead actor was Jean-Claude Van Damme. Howard had arranged for us to accommodate Jean-Claude's transportation needs during his stay in Pittsburgh.

I was introduced to Jean-Claude through Howard, and I was invited to many of the filming sets. The scene I remember most of all was when they opened up the famous dome of the Civic Arena, and the helicopter came flying out of the air and smashed onto the ice. They had filled the seats with cardboard "people" to make it look like the Civic Arena was full to capacity and a game was in progress. It was scary to see so many fire trucks and police present, just in case something went wrong. It was amazing to be a part of how that film was created, and then to watch the finished product was unbelievable.

I found Jean-Claude to be very friendly. During one of his breaks, he came to our office to meet the staff who had coordinated his transportation needs. He signed autographs and took pictures. He gave me the hat he was wearing, which had his name embroidered on it. I still have that hat as part of my collection.

Race Car Drivers

Mario Andretti

Michael Andretti

When Mario and Michael Andretti came to town to visit their family in Nazareth, Pennsylvania, both of them would always use my black-car services. I was introduced to the Andretti brothers by Chip Ganassi, a regular customer who owned race cars. Chip is a member of the Motorsports Hall of Fame of America.

WORLD WRESTLING FEDERATION

My mother with the World Wrestling belt

One of the most enjoyable services that Carriage Limousine provided was for the World Wrestling Federation (WWF). The reason why I say that is because my mother was a fan of all the wrestlers. Since we drove the wrestlers, I had the opportunity to get VIP front-row seats and backstage passes, making it possible for my mother to get pictures and autographs from the wrestlers. Some of the wrestlers she met that night included Macho Man Randy Savage, Razor Ramon, the Nasty Boys, and Sargent Slaughter, as well as the champion from Mount Lebanon, Pennsylvania, Kurt Angle.

KURT ANGLE

WWF WORLD WRESTLING FEDERATION

    Watching her cheering, screaming, and rooting for her favorites was priceless. To this day, I remember those moments like they just happened.

CHAPTER 9:
FIRST RETIREMENT

In late 2000, a major corporate client that frequently used our services became very interested in buying the company. After several phone calls and discussions during lunches and golf outings, we began negotiating a purchase contract. As these negotiations progressed, I realized that after building this company for several years, I wasn't ready to sell, and I discontinued the negotiations.

The CEO of the corporation, a very successful entrepreneur, still wanted to purchase my company. In May of the following year, he called and asked if he could send his accountant to my offices to handle the due diligence necessary for him to make a new offer that would work well for everyone involved. I directed him to my business attorney, who would create a document of confidentiality to verify the financials. Entrepreneurs are always looking for a good acquisition. He submitted a lowball offer to me; I told him I had no interest. I was flattered with his offer, but our numbers were too far apart.

About a month later, I met my attorney for lunch at the famous Common Plea restaurant. He told me that he had good news for me. He made me aware that the revised offer was twofold; it included the purchase of the company as well as an employment agreement paying $120,000 per year, with bonuses based upon mutually agreed profit-performance levels. My attorney thought this would be the perfect time to sell the business, based upon the fact that two new transportation companies were now operating in town, Uber and Lyft. Both were national companies, and this competition was beginning to affect my bottom line. Uber and Lyft were able to undercut my corporate business prices as well as my in-town car services. After a lot of thought, I saw this as the opportunity of a lifetime—I could run my company without having the financial responsibility of ownership. I would be doing what I do well: selling and managing my team. After we changed the licensing with the PUC, the ICC, and the operations entities at the Greater Pittsburgh International Airport into the names of the new owner, the sale was final.

I began my employment just as outlined in the contract. I would run the company, marketing and managing. I was very happy with my decision. After the first month, as most entrepreneurs do, they placed an accountant (a bean counter) in the office next to mine. He didn't understand the transportation business. He had no knowledge of the daily business decisions that I had made for the last fourteen years. He made it very difficult for me to operate in a positive, successful manner.

While the tension was growing between said accountant and me, I informed him that in January, I wanted to attend the annual limousine show in Los Angeles. This event was very informative. It made me aware of new ideas and events that could be used to help successfully grow and manage the business. It included marketing seminars and discussions of newer forms of transportation, and it introduced upgraded computer systems that were now available to our market. The show provided a valuable opportunity to network with many limousine company owners from different states and a chance to discuss how we could better meet the transportation needs of our clients. After we discussed this opportunity, I was informed that, based on the current sales and bottom line for the business, I would not be making the trip this year. I tried to explain that this is a twelve-month business that had high and low seasons. I told him that he was not making the right decision. Apparently, after being in the transportation business for four months, he was under the impression that he knew more about this business than I did with fourteen years of experience in running it!

Going back to my office that afternoon, I realized that the employment agreement situation was not going to work. I had always heard that often when companies are bought, changes must be made from management on down. Every day was a battle. I was watching a company that I had loved and nurtured beginning to crumble around me. Later that day, I went to the corporate office, had a meeting with the chairman, and resigned. When he asked why I wanted to resign, I proceeded to tell him that in four months, his accountant apparently felt he knew more about taking this company into the future than I had learned during the past fourteen years. The accountant was not taking any advice from me, he did not include me in making several major decisions, and I felt it was best to end the relationship. The chairman looked at me with astonishment and said, "You're making a mistake," and wished me well.

I then returned to my office on the South Side. As I was in the process of cleaning out my desk, the said accountant came in and asked me, "What do you think you're doing?" I informed him that I had just met with the chairman and had resigned and also that I had put in a very good word for him: "Since you know more than I do about how to run a successful transportation company, maybe he'll make you the new CEO." Just then, the phone in his office began ringing. I'm sure it was a call that he didn't want to answer.

As time went on, it was very clear that I made the right decision. I had shown that with a lot of hard work and team building, Carriage Limousine was always the number-one choice to provide clients with the first-class professional services they deserved. I was very blessed and had a lot of guidance from God. I enjoyed building a company on my own, starting from zero. I was given opportunities to meet many wonderful people, including celebrities, musicians, and sports figures.

CHAPTER 10:
CLOSING

Over the years, I've shared many of my stories with others, and I've often heard the comment, "You should write a book, and when you do, I want a copy."

I prepared this book during the COVID-19 pandemic. My wife, Kathy, and I live in McCandless, Pennsylvania, and were following our president's guidelines and sheltering at home. While much negativity was going on in the world, I was searching for something positive. I found myself sitting in my man cave and quietly reflecting on the many wonderful relationships, memories, and opportunities that I've had in my life. That's when I thought to myself, "Maybe it's time to write that book."

I believe this is the perfect time to share some of my great stories with everyone. And being the entrepreneur that I have always been, it makes me wonder: What will the next opportunity be?

I hope reading this book brings you some of the joy that I experienced while writing it during these trying times.

Enjoy,
Carl Gasper Jr.

ABOUT THE AUTHOR

I am seventy-four years young. During my life, I enjoyed owning a company that provided me with some wonderful and memorable experiences. In 2001, after fourteen years of hard work, twenty-four seven, 365 days a year, I retired from my business. I had many remarkable experiences and stories that I often shared with others. From time to time, my friends and acquaintances would say, "I want to hear more! You should write a book."

I think the time is right to share my stories with the world.

www.ingramcontent.com/pod-product-compliance
Lightning Source LLC
Chambersburg PA
CBHW050841050425
24652CB00033B/868